MW00488360

BEYOND THE DELTA

Critical Acclaim for *Beyond the Delta*

Beyond the Delta is an excellent sequence of life's questions that in David Brink's hands become thoughtful fun. His poems are both witty and kind. His wit does not cut; he finds the humor as well as the pathos in our human condition. Many of these poems evoke a wry smile and a "Yes!" deep down. He explores poetry's forms with grace. This poet is a man gone beyond all the nonsense, this is an elder sharing the wisdom he has earned. Read him. Learn.

—John Caddy, Poet, Naturalist, McKnight Artist of the Year

When David Brink found poetry, he found a perfect way to reflect, wonder and remember. *Beyond the Delta* is a record of a life's journey, and, in particular, how it feels to be the person one has always been but "In Disguise." "I'm masquerading as an aged man,/ "Whose face is framed in chalk-white hair and beard," he says. Brink poses big questions, and he answers them with honesty and humor, taking us from age five to ninety in a single poem. It's a pleasure to read these wonderfully varied and always interesting poems, and to wish the author well "Beyond the delta's farthest sands."

—Joyce Sutphen, Poet Laureate of Minnesota

Those who have been waiting for David Brink's first collection of poems to appear will be delighted by the publication of *Beyond the Delta*... The poems are devoted to many topics presented in wide varieties of forms and styles, ranging from verses touching on ancient subjects to tightly executed wit, to powerfully emotional narratives and portraits of characters caught in emotional binds, as well as tales and monologues tightly presented with taut language and vivid imagery... Myth, history, and personal experience unite to keep our attention focused on the world of experience and the world of rhetoric and ideas, all woven together with great skill...What a long-awaited and brilliant debut!... Brink has a polymath's ability to explain, to engage the reader's affection and intelligence, and to charm language lovers with his precision, his wit, and his emotional and intellectual freshness...

—John Calvin Rezmerski, Poet and Teacher

To Katharine, with best wishes, David R. Brink

BEYOND THE DELTA

POEMS

DAVID RYRIE BRINK

MILL CITY PRESS | MINNEAPOLIS, MN

Copyright © 2016 by David Ryrie Brink

Mill City Press, Inc.
322 First Avenue N, 5th floor
Minneapolis, MN 55401
612.455.2293
www.millcitypublishing.com

All rights reserved. No part of this publication may be reproduced, stored in a retrieval system, or transmitted, in any form or by any means, electronic, mechanical, photocopying, recording, or otherwise, without the prior written permission of the author.

ISBN-13: 978-1-63413-763-8
LCCN: 2015920147

Book Design by E. Keene

Printed in the United States of America

In memory of my parents,
Carol Ryrie Brink and Raymond Woodard Brink,
To whom I owe life and the love of words.

Contents

II - Now and Then / 23

III - Love and Loss / 41

IV - Rants and Chants / 67

About the Author / 89

Author's Note

A few of these poems have been published in periodicals, but most appear here for the first time.

I am solely responsible for any lapse of skill or taste in this little collection. But I am grateful to friends, family and some fellow poets for suggestions and encouragement. And I must acknowledge, with special gratitude, comments from Jeff Shotts, the late Susan Hauser, J. T. Caddy, Joyce Sutphen, John C. Rezmerski and Connie Wanek, among others. I am particularly indebted to David P. Murrin for his piece About the Author, to June Blumenson who reviewed all the poems and made extensive suggestions and to Carol Schullo for her faithful transcription of my text and her guidance in electronic matters.

In writing these poems, I have been guided by my basic canon that poetry is a form of communication from poet to reader. That does not mean that it cannot be beautiful, mysterious, figurative, allusive, strange or comic. What it does mean is that its language should be clear and intelligible to the reader. I try to avoid the cryptic and inaccessible that characterizes some of today's poetry. While the decline of public interest in poetry today primarily results from the rise of electronic and other diversions, it may also be true that poetry has moved away from the people more than the people have moved away from poetry.

In the current age, I do not feel we can afford to disqualify any types, styles or subjects of poetry. Meter, rhyme and forms (such as sonnets or ballads) can add to the beauty, wit or memorability of poetry. But, of course, they should not be allowed to obscure the poem's meaning. And often only free verse can adequately express a mood, picture or idea without distraction. As a consequence, the reader will find in this book a wide range of subjects in a variety of styles, meters, rhymes, forms and free verse.

Enjoy!

                                    - DRB
                                    Minneapolis, Minnesota

I

Here and There

My heart leaps up when I behold
     A rainbow in the sky;
So was it when my life began;
So is it now I am a man;
So be it when I shall grow old,
     Or let me die!
The child is the father of the man;
And I could wish my days to be
Bound each to each by natural piety.

-- Wordsworth

The Voyage

So soon our tiny craft is launched
Upon the river's teeming flood,
To toss and twist as wills the stream,
While those who launched us drift away
Or disappear in eddied swells,
And leave us without motive force
To sail upstream, reversing course,
Yet strength to dock at ports of call.

And so we stop at many ports –
Some ports of learning, ports of work,
And ports of friendship, ports of love,
And ports of help, of parenthood.
But many ports along the way
We pass, aware we can't return.

So long the trip, so slow the stream,
So many ports unvisited.
And, in the end, so much alone,
Until, at last, we reach the sea –
Beyond the delta's farthest sands
And float the limitless unknown.

Sunday Morning

This Sunday morning, going to the lake,
I took a narrow road with dappled sun
Becoming a cathedral, high and green,
Made up of gothic arches, as the trees
From either side conjoined to make the ribs
That formed the lofty columns, vault and nave,
Aglow with beams surpassing fine stained glass,
And, at a transept, windows flaming gold.

At last I reached a clearing, like an apse.
With deep celestial blue of lake and sky,
That formed an altar for my Sunday rites –
A brighter one than those of wood and stone…
I had my church, my altar and this creed
From Pope: *The proper study of mankind*
Is man, to which, in my sincere belief,
I'd add: …*and every thing that's in his scope.*

"The Child is the
Father of the Man"
from Wordswoth

How to explain a human being?
No, the answer is not just in a microscope,
Nor in a periodic table of elements or
Magnetic resonance imaging;
They leave untouched life's central mysteries.

How did you move from your
Role as Observer to your role as Actor –
The Actor, the *only* actor in your play?
How did you come by your *You*-ness –
Your unique identity?

Why were you chosen to fill a term
As this particular human being
On this particular planet,
Of this particular solar system
And in this particular galaxy?

How did you happen to fit inside this skin,
Look out these eye-holes, feel pain,
Interact with what you find here;
Live, feel love, procreate and die,
Leaving the cosmos imperceptibly changed?

Yes, it's true that everything is connected.
But such are the permutations and
Combinations of life's building blocks
That, even though cloned, your being
Will never quite be duplicated.

And so, from being born without clothes,
Without knowledge, thought or history,
You start with a totally blank scroll.
But instantly begin to record on it your
Feelings, hopes, experiences, loves and hates.

You acquire traits from myriad forebears,
And spend your early years at home,
Heredity and experience both shape you,
And, in turn, you'll pass them on.
And so the child becomes the father of the man.

Our Mother

The sea, the sea!
Mother of all life
Upon our unique orb;
Everlasting, she outlives
Her earthly creatures.
And, as all the glaciers
And the permafrost
Thaw out and flow,
She rises once again to
Reclaim her offspring,
Vegetable and animal,
Resorbed into the great womb
From which they issued forth.

The Scale of Things

A colony of ants lives busily
At the back of my back yard,
Believing it owns the world.
To an ant I could be God,
Beneficent or vengeful –
Unseen, but all-powerful –
Capable of harboring or destroying
The ant, or its entire colony,
With water, fire or chemicals,
Or by the casual imprint of my boot.

But I am not a sudden storm,
An unimagined force of nature,
Or unforeseeable Act of God.
And I am not, nor is my world,
The nucleus or center of the Universe…
Whose ant, do you suppose, am I?

Dark Matter

Life is the little Span
Between the Unconsciousness
Of the Before
And the Unconsciousness
Of the After.

Our Life –
So Precious
To us Now;
So Meaningless
When it has flickered out.

We then exist
Only in the Memory
Of the Survivors –
While they Survive
And have Memory.

Only a few Human Works
Survive Memory –
The Monuments
And Detritus
Of our Sojourn.

Man has a fierce
Desire to Live;
Mankind has a fierce
Determination to
Destroy Itself.

And What shall remain
When the Relics
Of our Passage –
The Edifices and the DNA –
Are swallowed in the Black Hole?

How to Pray

Mankind has prayed, it would appear,
As long as we have been on earth;
At first to spirits haunting *things*
And animals or elements,
And then, to hosts of unseen gods
Who regulate affairs of men.

At last, belief began to gel,
Throughout the world of modern man,
That there is but a single God –
All-powerful, creator, judge,
All-knowing and benevolent,
To whom our prayers should be addressed.

And yet, despite our countless prayers,
The good die young – or they die old.
Some rascals meet with punishment,
While others gather huge rewards.
And men fight men for land or gold,
Or, often, their belief in God.

We know disease and poverty,
Injustice and catastrophe,
And these seem tempered only by
The work of diligent mankind.
Does God not hear, or care to act?
Then why do we continue prayer?

My pious grandma used to say
That God helps those who help themselves.
The great Serenity Prayer
Attempts to teach the simple truth:
What *we* can't change, we must accept.
And so we learn in our own prayers

To pray for things that *we* can change.
A prayer to win the lottery
Will not increase our chance of luck.
To wish our mate will be more kind
Will never work by prayer alone,
But personal commitment might.

We find that prayer will not change God.
It changes only those who pray.
We cannot change outside events,
But can commit *ourselves* to change.
Commitment's strongest form is prayer
A solemn promise to ourselves,

And others, public or alone.
Some say the vow must be to God.
But others pray in private words
Of personal commitment, or
Confession, praise or gratitude,
Without invoking any god.

Danger in Poetry

As men and women seek success in love
And covet youth and long fertility,
So poets pray their patron muse above
For grants of endless immortality.
They seek it in a thousand different ways;
Some try to write in metric verse and rhyme,
While some prefer the free and unrhymed phrase,
And all experiment from time to time.

Some poets seem to seek their opposite.
Old poets write of youth and love's hot breath
And all remembered joys they will admit.
The younger write of age's pangs and death.
They seem to dwell on death and be obsessed
And, all too often, end – by it possessed.

Questioning Dylan

"Do not go gentle into that good night,"
Said Dylan Thomas' villanelle adept.
Today we ponder what advice is right.

So must we rage against the dying light
Before our everlasting sleep is slept –
And not go gentle into that good night?

Or rather the Serenity Prayer recite:
And things we cannot change come to accept?
Today we ponder what advice is right.

When hospice care allays the deathbed plight
And serves to stem the force of wrath inept –
Do not go gentle into that good night?

With every sense about to take its flight,
Should this, our final hour, be raged and wept?
Today we ponder what advice is right.

Should we accept the dying of the light
And gentle go in ancient dreams well-kept,
Or not go gentle into that good night?
Today we ponder what advice is right.

Cogito

I went to see the wise man in his cave,
To ask the meaning of it all.
When I called out,
He came forth from within
And sat crosslegged
Before the mouth of the cave.

After a pause, the wise man said:
First, I must ask for your response:
All generalizations are false, including this.
I thought, and then I said:
I think it means some generalizations are true.
But isn't that itself a generalization? he asked.

And then he asked if I could square the circle,
To that I answered, *There are squares larger*
And squares smaller than a given circle.
So I conclude that somewhere in between
The square and circle must be equal.—
Yes, but try to state the formula for
The equality of all squares and circles.

And he further paused and then asked,
Give me a case of perpetual motion.
To which I answered, *Gravity is perpetual motion.*
But consider this, the wise man said,
Gravity attracts an object to a mass,
But when the object meets the mass,
Does not the object come to rest?

To which I quickly gave reply:
I'm not sure Newton would agree with that.
Nor I, nor Einstein either, the wise man said.
And then he further spoke:
We are but pygmies, standing on the shoulders
Of other pygmies, to try to see the truth.
And what we cannot well explain
Some men have come to say is God.
But every thing is knowable.

Every thing has a cause.
And every thing is related,
Whether proximately or remotely,
To every other thing.

And then the wise man slowly
Rose, turned and disappeared
Into the recesses of his cave.
And I knew I would learn no more.

Aliens Among Us

Where did they come from?
How did they get here?
What is it that they want?
How did they so cleverly
Assume our shapes, our clothes,
Our dwellings and our lives,
Mingling among us undetected
Except by their views and actions?
It is only thus that we know them.

They oppose what we have built,
Denying evolution, global warming;
Refusing vaccination for their children,
The freedom to worship or not worship;
Denying responsibility for the environment;
Opposing any government whatsoever;
Declining the cost of the common good;
Opposing the will of the majority;
Caring much for themselves and little for others.

They oppose the basic rights of women
And their freedom from violence
Or to control their own bodies;
Killing in the name of right to life;
Hating those of different color or belief;
Restricting, when they can, the right to vote;
Insisting that the way to peace and safety
Is to arm all persons against all others;
Denouncing all the arts and education
As elitist and corrupt.

Were these strange creatures
Expelled from another planet?
Or from some bygone age...?
It does not greatly matter.
For it is our policy and our law
To let the aliens live in peace
Among us and let them vote,
And insist upon their views;
We let them mingle freely,
Let them merge and breed.
We are left with only hope
That, at some future time,
They will join our civilization.

On Second Thought

I tread across the green gully,
Along a faint rough track,
Through a dense growth of myrtle.

Ahead I see a little clutch
Of tiny newborn snakes
Wriggle across the footpath.

Already their triangle heads
Tell me they could grow up
To kill me on this murky path.

Now I could stamp them out,
But something makes me pause –
And then hurry on my way.

Green myrtle closes up behind.
Darkness slowly trickles in
To fill the basin of the gully.

Scattered Pages

Ah Poetry, that slender waif,
Beset by fickle winds of chance,
Her labored leaves no longer safe,
But lost to breezes' frenzied dance.

As so much beauty wafts afar,
Perhaps to burial in the sea
Or drifting ever like a star
To seek an unknown destiny,

May errant winds reverse their course
And blow back every missing page,
Restored to Poetry, their source,
So needed in a prosaic age.

Thanks Be

I have tasted boundless joy and sorrow.
I've known times of love and times of hate,
Times of health and times of sickness,
Times with friends and some with foes,
Times of ease and some of poverty,
In settings both beautiful and ugly.

But I am steeped in gratitude for all –
Whether good or bad is almost meaningless –
Happy that by some unlikely chance
I was propelled here from the void
To be – for this tiny slice of eternal time,
A passenger on Earth's cosmic flight.

I Aspire

For this present time and for the time to come
May I wash clean all traces of the past,
Flush out the source of every poisoned thought –
Resentments, hates, jealousies and fears,
Mistakes, regrets for whatever might-have-beens,
Bias, lies, cruelties, disputes, unthinking words.

And let me rub out every future wrong,
Each coming smudge of worry, fears,
Envy, sloth and wasteful fruitless dreams,
Until the freight I've caused myself to bear
Has gone like writing from a new-washed slate.
Leaving bare the consciousness and ready will.

And then let thought and action drift back in,
Like the incoming, flooding, morning tide,
As it draws and leaves new patterns on the sand.
And let my will and life force begin anew,
With fresh impressions and new resolves,
Without aim, except to live the good and true.

II
Now and Then

An aged man is but a paltry thing,
A tattered coat upon a stick, unless
Soul clap its hands and sing, and louder sing
For every tatter in its mortal dress.

-- Yeats

In Disguise

I pass my days in deep assumed disguise.
I'm masquerading as an aged man
Whose face is framed in chalk-white hair and beard,
A trifle slow afoot and somewhat stooped.

Inside, I'm still a youthful cavalier,
Romantic, bright and full of jealousy,
With quick response to challenges or slights,
Renowned for prowess vast in love and war.

But, once in my disguise, my feelings change.
I'm now forgetful, gentle, wise and kind,
Appreciating fellow travelers –
My kindred, all, upon this little earth.

And those who meet me seem to like my mask.
They favor it beyond the real me.
I've slowly grown attached to it myself;
I think I'll wear it to my end of days.

Our Alchemy

How glorious our planet's gift of seasons.
A world of strange, mysterious alchemy,
Whereby the humble pussy willow changes
From catkins' silver into floral gold,
The caterpillar to the chrysalis,
The chrysalis to the butterfly.

The hidden chemistry that rules us all,
By which we live through all our seasons:
Spring, verdant with all youthful hope;
Summer, in its full vigor and ecstasy,
Autumn, rich in harvest, touched with gall,
And Winter's static days of ripe maturity.

At last, all seasons end and pass away
That every thing may come to be re-born,
And bring, once more, a pussy willow crop,
The lowly caterpillar's future bright,
And our own magic metamorphosis,

A Faerie Ring

Our tour bus stopped beside an Irish wood.
We all got out to view an old stockade.
Most gathered 'round the place our tour guide stood,
But, on beyond, I glimpsed a sunlit glade,
And, inside me, I heard a drumming sound
That called me to the glade – a faerie ring
Of mossy stones just seen above the ground.
And, silently, my heart began to sing
A wild, enchanted song not heard before,
And I began a strange druidic dance,
My body swaying 'round the dancing floor.
But soon I sensed another's vivid glance –
A woman tourist shared my silent beat,
With auburn hair, green eyes and dancing feet.

Time's Pace

When I was five,
Time scarcely moved.
It seemed forever –
'Til Christmas,
My birthday
Or starting school.
A year – one slow fifth
Of all the life I knew.

When I was fifteen,
Everything life held
Seemed still to come –
Driving a car,
Loving someone,
Belonging somewhere.
Ever the youngest person
In the entire room.

When I was forty-five
Was this all? Yet
Never time enough
To pay the bills
Or tend the family
Or pursue my career.
Could I now go back
To age, perhaps, fifteen?

When I was ninety
Years flew by like days...
I needed still a little time –
Remembering friends,
Planning final touches,
Writing my Obit.
Ever the oldest person
In the entire room

Early Moments

I. Bliss–I Am Six

My parents went to run an errand
At a farm well beyond our lake.
We took a little rutted road.
They let me wander by myself.

I crossed into a high meadow
Framed around by dark green woods
From which I could see the very tip
Of our lake and, beyond, two lakes more.

I sat down in deep ripe prairie grass –
Timothy, broomsedge and wild rye,
With blue flags and sailors, yellow daisies,
Standing slightly higher than my eyes.

A gentle breeze wafted from the south.
The air was soft and somewhat humid
Wrapping as warmly around me
As my mother's circling arms.

Time stood still; I knew no care.
I wanted nothing but that moment.
Happiness was implicit in the scene
With nothing lacking from perfection.

I now can't find that lovely meadow.
The road and field must have changed,
But with the lapse of over ninety years,
The image lasts unchanged and bright.

II. The Librarian – I Am Ten

Plump, bright and eager, the librarian –
The stacks of books her only family –
Yearned for meaning and connection,
And loved to visit often at our house.

She openly worshipped my warm, creative mother –
Writer of books, artist and friend to so many.
And, I suspect, she secretly desired my tall Father –
Professor, mathematician and universal sage.

At one of many dinners at our home,
While my parents were busy in the kitchen,
She looked my way, smiled faintly
And, seeking something to say, asked:

"How does it feel to be a perfectly ordinary
Boy with two such wonderful parents?"
I don't now remember what I answered,
But never in my life forgot the question.

III. Witness – I Am Twelve

A number of us boys and girls
Are climbing higher on the mountain
Than the school from which we came.
Across the valley behind us we see
Taller mountains' snowy, jagged peaks.

Most of the group are looking up toward
Our mountain's rounded top – our goal.
But I see a tiny trickle from a spring
Sliding down a nearly white limestone wall.
At its base I see a small stalagmite forming;

And, on the sides, layers of sediment
Building a new generation of white stone,
Still so soft that I can separate
The layers with my fingers.
And there I find perfect impressions –

Of leaves, of a beetle and a snail
The originals already rotted away and gone.
These are fossils at their very birth.
I feel that I'm standing at the beginning
Of our earth – a witness to the creation!

Astronomy 101

Our place in the universe –
A thought that challenged me.

Through school and books
I learned that Earth is not

The center of the universe
Nor is our star, the sun,

Nor even our own galaxy,
We call the Milky Way…

A harder lesson by far –
I am not the center of the

Universe, nor sun, nor earth.
Little revolves around me.

My lesson then is to accept
That I am but a minute speck

In the total cosmic scheme;
And, assuredly, I am not God.

Geriatrics

Old age is rotten:
You lose your muscle,
Lose your precious potency,
Lose your sense of balance,
Lose some of your good health,
Lose some recent memory,
Lose some great countrymen,
Lose many dearly-loved people.
Yes, it's a rotten time.

But, then, you do gain some things.
You gain appreciation of others,
Gain a lifetime of fond memories
Gain the power to admit you're wrong,
Gain freedom from pretense,
Gain the power to ask for help,
Gain understanding of yourself,
Maybe not such a bad deal!
Just wish it lasted longer.

A Certain Light

The warm light just before the sun sets,
Like the glow sent out by molten steel,
Casts long shadows across the lawn –

Shadows of great trees, and human figures
Standing still as trees, and seeming placed
Precisely by some divine engraver –

Each figure with a purpose and a meaning,
As actors posed in some cosmic tableau.
And, when the light fades slowly, blending

Dull mixtures of orange, green and purple,
The image lingers in its original colors,
Graven on our limbic consciousness

Spring Comes North

For us, the children of the North,
Our April brings its tardy pledge,
That May redeems and quickly claims
As landscapes morph from brown to green.

The offspring of our ancient trees
Appear again as feathery shoots
And limbs adorned with pastel blooms
As tender as a newborn babe.

The tired and the left-for-dead
Still harbor resurrection's seed
That sprouts again perennial hope
That youth may live eternally.

As love may be most keenly felt
By those who've had and lost a love;
Or full enjoyment of good health
Be valued most by those once ill,

So, for us dwellers of the North,
Our Spring is welcome all the more
Because it follows on the heels
Of unremitting icy cold.

Two Faces

A face – so young, so bright and still unlined
And looking ever forward, daring all,
In search of new events and states of mind
Beyond the present or beyond recall.

Another face – so weathered, strong and tan,
Surveying everything that's in the past,
Reviewing all events since time began
And seeking to relive their vista vast.

A man lives now and in the coming days.
Through life he'll change and wear the other face.
In passing time he'll come to look both ways,
As one face by the other he'll replace.

Thus Everyman may gain a double view,
And Janus, two-faced god, be found in you.

Dealing with Age

With age our eyes film over,
Ears stuff up with cotton,
Skin folds like an accordion,
Muscles dry into leather,
Bones brittle as candy canes,
Stature bends and shrinks,
Pain our frequent companion.
Slow minds still outstrip energy.
We borrow from tomorrow
Until tomorrow doesn't come.

Some live on in misery,
Waiting for hereafter's bliss.
Some keep on through obligation,
Duty's shackles holding them.
Some swim the quiet seas of doubt –
Half in hope and half in fear.
Some can't face the horrid slope;
Let them go then, let them go....
But some find the fact of being
Still more joyous than the void.

River Voices

Brooklets surging, freshets merging,
Waters springing, rivers singing,
Discords ended, voices blended:

Lackawanna, Susquehanna,
Shenandoah, Cuyahoga,
Mississippi, Tennessee.

Tallahatchee, Allegheny,
Androscoggin, Namekagon,
Chattahootchee, Kankakee.

Rappahannock, Housatonic,
Piscataqua, Escanaba,
Michigammi, Genessee.

Music flowing, onward going,
Tones harmonic, chords symphonic,
River voices – earth rejoices.

Toward the Light

Our hopeful race seeks ever-brighter light –
A candle, lantern, beacon, guiding ray.
Some glimpse it on the old year's darkest night;
Some see it on the new year's brightest day.

As Akhenaten found his god – the Sun,
Or Homer sang of burning Troy agleam,
Or Shakespeare penned his lines so brightly done,
Or Einstein discovered particles in a beam.

Such heroes dazzle with their brilliant blaze,
But we must strike our own uncertain spark,
To try to fire a torch to light our days
And lead us through their gloom, however dark,

That we may never fall or go astray,
But find and follow our own shining way.

III
Love and Loss

Sometimes I dream awake.
Sometimes I see her face
in its strong-featured beauty —
with her eyes full of pity.

-- Donald Hall

Petals

A beauty still at sixty years –
Her birthday gift, a single rose,
As red as blood and full and fair,
At last a wilting petal fell,
And thence each day she gently stripped
A drying petal from the core
So that the rose again stood tall,
And young and lovely once again,
But yet more slim and graceful still.

Then came a love into her life,
Another rose so full and fair.
And lest it ever fade and droop,
She stripped off jealousy and hate,
  Next cast off fear and futile pride
And, lastly, empty schemes and masks.
And thus she grew a second life
In which she gloried, strong and tall,
And yet more slim and graceful still

The House

In travel to my summer lodge
I pass a tiny town –
A crossroad of antiquity,
Its houses gray and brown.

One house, once elegant, stands out,
For want of paint and care,
Its roof askew, its fences down,
For animals a lair.

And when I met, and wed, my love,
At once she felt its charm.
She wanted that deserted house
And saw no hint of harm.

She said it was her "haunted house".
She longed to meet the ghosts
Who dwelt within, and we'd delight
To entertain as hosts.

Said she, "The price should not be high.
I'd gladly give my purse.
Back taxes might suffice"...Said I,
"There's no investment worse."

And so we lived without her house,
That single wish denied,
Until the unexpected day
When, suddenly, she died.

And now her house is falling down.
It's haunted now at last.
And my investment in that house
Has grown to something vast.

Facing Reality

When Death contrived to steal my love.
He took from me a part.
I did not realize it then,
But now, I miss my heart.

My life rolls on, quite weightlessly,
Devoid of heavy care.
It's now, for want of gravity,
A cloud adrift in air.

I wish I had the faith to think
Some day we'd reunite
And, in some far celestial place,
Regain our old delight.

I cannot entertain such hope,
For reason is my curse.
I'm wed now to reality –
For better or for worse.

Brutus

Ten men trapped Brutus
In the far lowland jungle
Of East Central Africa
They brought him out to
A big American zoo

They put Brutus behind
Bars and a panel of heavy glass.
Brutus was a prime attraction –
Glistening black with silver on his back
Six hundred pounds of muscle.

Brutus mainly sat morose
And glowered, with seeming hate,
At all those humans who daily
Crowded against the rail that
Kept them from his glass.

Then one day Brutus stood erect
Looking out from his glass
And gazed at Flora, tall and blond,
A member of the human crowd.
Brutus seemed to beckon her.

And so she came to the rail
Brutus put out his great hands
Pressed flat against the glass,
Inviting Flora to match his
Offered hand to hand

Challenged and unafraid ,
Flora slipped beneath the rail
And put her hands against Brutus' –
Separated only by the glass
And so they stood in long communion.

The crowd fell back amazed
At this show of love and harmony.
And some said that Brutus smiled.
At last an officer of the zoo
Made Flora step back behind the rail.

And people later said that Brutus
Paid no attention to anyone else,
But seemed always to be looking
Sadly, for his partner Flora,
Apparently wanting no one else.

When Flora returned some weeks later
Brutus moved quickly to the glass,
Putting his hands against it.
Once more she matched hers with his
And, again, he seemed somehow content.

The next year Flora moved away
And, to all his loyal fans, Brutus
Seemed to fade and be depressed.
It was in that next year
That Brutus unexpectedly died.

Mutation

When we first met,
Like starving wolves; we
Fell instantly upon each other,
Panting with passion,
Torrid and feral,
Using any floor or wall
As bed and springboard,
Until, gasping and exhausted
We fell back satisfied.

And we were very sure
We'd found the whole aim of life.
And so we journeyed on.
You and I obsessed,
Until, at last, we came
Upon a stunning roadblock:
Malignancy, radiation and the knife.
Then, for a time, we thought
Our life together was over.

But, facing the reality,
We began to find a new kind
Of mutual satisfaction
That lasted beyond
The next morning.
And then one day I knew
We had discovered love,
Something richer and deeper
Than we had known before.

Croquet

He, a scholar, loved all games
And played to win,
Extracting every nuance
Of skill and strategy,

While She, a writer
And an artist,
Born to be creative,
Was all impulse.

When partners in croquet
He'd plot and scheme
And make each shot
Carefully and cleverly,

He'd leave the ball
In the correct position,
Then show her how
To make the perfect shot.

Soon she'd tire of this,
And cry: "It's just a game!"
And give the ball a wild whack
While He near had a stroke.

He'd usually find
Another way to win.
He was gifted musically,
Knew everything.

She could put down
The vacuum cleaner
And write another chapter
Or paint a watercolor.

She had a flair with people
And always a helping hand.
She knew all birds
And wildflowers.

He could solve any equation,
Inspire a classroom,
Draw plans for anything,
Give sound advice.

Through the alchemy of love,
Somehow they made
A strange and perfect
Blend of unmatched souls.

Granny Goodyear Explains

Yes, my dear, and now you want to know
Why men and women are so different?...
Well, it's all about what's called testosterone.
And everybody's got a bit, of course,
But men have got the biggest load by far.
It makes them just exactly what they are:
So big and strong and rough and clad in hair,
Combative, crude and always hot for love
They dream of girls and sex both day and night
And measure life by how much they may get.

Not that we pious women are immune,
We like to flirt with tall and handsome men
Broad in chest and shoulders, tight in buns.
And skillful guys can really get us going.
But mostly we believe in fairy tales;
We think we're cast as princess in the play
And that Prince Charming will ride off with us
And we'll live happily forever after
In the palace or rose-covered house
With many happy, decent, handsome kids.

When first we meet the prince and fall in love,
We catch the fever, want love and sex
As much, or more, than even any man.
But we, as women, cannot keep it up;
We don't have quite enough testosterone.
We find he's just a man and not a prince.
Our fever cools and interest lags a bit,
Which men can never understand at all.

And so they go out looking once again.
Although they may be trying to stay true
To us, to home and everything we want,
The pressure of the glands is just too much.

Now please don't misunderstand me.
I'm not defending men who go astray
I'm only trying to explain the facts
Of how testosterone operates – in all of us;
Sometimes the source of very frightful things
It can cause rapes and other sorts of crime.
It starts domestic violence and wars,
It feeds on feuds and fights and rivalries.

But testosterone is not forever bad.
Without it, we might not exist at all
And we might miss the joys of a shared life.
Some say perhaps we'd live in trees or caves –
But they might be filled with curtains and blooms –
The woman's endocrine touch at work.
Our woman's testosterone must live with men's,
To insure our human race still breeds
To keep existence and evolving life
Upon this little planet we call home
And now, my dear, Granny's got to go.
She's got a date – a really cute new guy.

The Dog

The accommodating dog who brought ten thousand sticks
Because he understood how much you enjoyed
Throwing them and watching him bring them back.
He thought you'd never tire of that sport.

The faithful dog who watched the baby carriage,
And bristled when an unknown person approached,
But relaxed when you told him it was a friend.
Still, no stranger could have touched your wife or child.

The careful dog who warned you of suspicious things.
Even though he knew barking irritated you,
He felt he must never fail in his solemn duty,
Whether it turned out to be popular or not.

The guilty dog who slunk around contritely,
Not needing any punishment at all from you,
When, being left behind from the picnic trip,
In his first resentment he had chewed your shoe.

The member-of-the family dog whose every action
Said he couldn't possibly get along without you.
And you had to lock him up when you left,
Because, however far you went, he'd try to go.

The patient dog who suffered incurable cancer
In silence, bearing pain that had to be immense,
Who tried and tried to come to you, but fell,
His once swift legs unable to sustain him.

And, on his final trip, the apologetic dog
You lifted to the passenger seat of the car, where,
Despite his fear and pain, his eyes said plainly "Sorry...
Don't worry, it's not your fault."

Ghosts

They steal in, singly or in a chorus
Of diverse shades – some quite large,
Some small, some in pastel colors,
Some bright as neon, some vague as fog.

At times, I hear them gently chant,
Whisper, orate, babble, murmur,
Audible, not quite intelligible,
Yet sometimes clear in implication.

Faces to which I cannot put a name,
Old failures from a case, or love, I lost,
A person I deserted or lied to,
Slandered or could have helped.

When I try to make amends
The ghost may fade or disappear.
But another ghost is always ready
To move in to fill a vacancy.

My Love

Today I had a sudden urge to call
Just to say, "Missing you. I love you.
I'm so lucky to be part of your life."

So then I call, and you want to know why
I'm calling…and then you tell me your friend's
Ex-husband died and what his symptoms were.

You tell me that the sink still drips,
And that you're distressed about the
Situation in Kyrgyzstan and about the Tea Party.

Then I put my hand briefly over the phone,
Because my assistant wants urgently to know
To whom we should send copies of my letter.

It turns out I missed a question on the phone.
"You never really listen to me," you say…
Next time, I'll wait and bring flowers home.

The Second Sex–Redux

(after Simone de Beauvoir - Le Deuxieme Sexe - 1949)

I.

Oh, great Simone, how well and true you spoke,
Just more than half a century ago,
In saying women were the second sex.
You told the lot of women of that time
And also those of every age before.

For centuries the men, in all their strength
And overweening lust and angry pride,
Would battle nature, beasts and other men
To dominate, possess and rule the world,
Including all that famous second sex.

Indeed, those were the glory days of men.
While women, pregnant, overworked,
Beset with hosts of seldom-wanted babes,
Were kept from learning and heroic roles,
And made to think they'd earned their hapless lot.

Simone found matters just about the same,
Surveying life in nineteen forty-nine.
For women still made up "the other" sex –
The mistress, wife or daughter of some man,
With self-hood just beyond their failing grasp.

II.

Then, suddenly, some things began to change
And seemed to come together all at once:
With legalized abortion and the Pill,
Desegregation aiding civil rights,
And shorter weeks and daily hours of work

Employment openings that came with wars,
Appliances, prepared and frozen foods,
A life in suburbs with a second car,
With power steering, automatic shift,
Machines all run by nature's energy.

The world of global change we live in now
Does not require the special strengths of men
In combat, force, aggression or debate.
Today we need the arts that women long have used:
Communication and collaboration.

III.

Now women lead a life of ample choice,
They choose if they will bear a child or not.
They practice every calling, every trade,
Profession, business, sport or military force,
As principals and leaders – not just help.

Today more women are employed than men,
More women seeking education now
At every level, college or graduate,
Research and business, medicine or law,
Their presence strengthens every discipline.

Most men are glad to share what was their sphere,
Accepting women partners as their peers.
But still some cannot seem to understand
Or notice changes coming every day,
And thus impede the progress of our world…

IV.

Simone would surely change her mind today.
She might envision an unfolding scene
Embracing vistas of approaching time
When women run the most important work
While men play roles of help or special tasks:

With women dominant in art and trade
And education, health, research,
And every kind of people skill;
Then men might serve as soldier, athlete, coach,
Or entertainer, laborer or police.

Ah yes, Simone today no doubt would say
It's men who have become the second sex…
But being also very wise and fair
She'd want the world better as a whole,
And so she'd add: "Allons, Allons, les Hommes!"

Leo's Pride

The splendid alpha male lion
Is ruler of the total pack.
So handsome is his shaggy mane,
So awesome is his mighty roar.

"The King of Beasts," you likely say.
Think once again, is my reply.

The females hunt and chase and kill.
They feed the cubs, their young.
They beat off wild dogs and crocs
And keep a watch throughout the night.

"Just Female Work," you might assert.
It's work for all, it seems to me.

The male breeds and breeds again
And drives the others from the kill.
And when his hunger and his lust are slaked,
He sleeps and then he sleeps some more.

"A *Pride* of Lions" you could observe.
More surely a *Disgrace*, I'd say.

J S B

Prolific Johann Sebastian Bach
Surpassed his peers in productivity:
Chorales, partitas, canons, oratorios
Concertos, masses, preludes, suites, sonatas;
Composed a new cantata every week.
He sang, composed and played
And taught all instruments.
Considered rather great in his own day,
But greater still in each succeeding age.
Today he's widely thought to be the best.

The very soul of creativity,
His second cousin was his starter wife.
He sired seven children from that wife.
When she wore out and sadly passed away.
He wed a second wife, both young and strong,
And with that wife begot a second brood
Thus adding to the seven, thirteen more –
A total sum of twenty boys and girls –
A large and musically gifted group
He taught with rigor all his art and skill.
Indeed prodigious, Bach, in every way.

Among the children who survived and grew,
The girls, as was the custom of that day,
All used their gift for pious churchly song.
But all the boys composed and played in public.
They used initials to keep the record straight.
The eldest was William Friedemann Bach,
(Thus WFB); and CPE Bach,
Perhaps the greatest; JGB Bach,
And GHB, and also JCFB,
And last of all the sons, JCB,
For Johann Christian Bach, another great.

All fine composers, players and fine men.
Each in his own right should be revered,
And yet, most failed of everlasting fame,
Forever tagged as merely "Sons of Bach",
(Or, in that self-same spirit, SOB's)
Condemned to stand in ever-darkening shade
Of the giant, fecund figure, JSB...
So hard to be a son with other letters.

Almost

Today he looked inside a dusty trunk,
Inspected every unworn shirt and suit –
Some bought too small or later washed and shrunk
Or put aside for reasons now quite moot.
Plus some a size or two too long or wide
Mementos of old grandiosity,
From yesterdays of hope and naïve pride
And youthful certitude and vanity.

He then thought through the dusty trunk of life:
Salutatorian in his senior term;
His second choice of girls became his wife;
And then Vice Chairman of his legal firm.
He finished runner-up in many a post
And slowly learned acceptance – well, almost.

The Guest

He first arrived the day we met.
We knew when he appeared
He spelled a danger and a threat
Of everything we feared.

We did not want to let him win;
We locked and barred the gate.
But somehow he kept getting in –
A messenger of fate.

At last he entered in to stay;
He was our constant guest.
He came to rule our lives each day
And bring us joy and rest.

And soon we knew beyond a doubt,
Like living vital parts,
The guest we could not live without
Was one with both our hearts.

We thought some day we would have flown
Together to our grace,
But fate chose one to go alone
And one to stay in place.

The one that now must stay behind
Is really not alone,
Because there dwells within his mind
The guest we made our own.

IV
Rants and Chants

True, I talk of dreams,
Which are the children of an idle brain,
Begot of nothing but vain fantasy

-- Shakespeare

Encounters–Three Scenes

I

When Shakespeare entered *The Bull and Boar*
He saw it was already too late to avoid
Marlowe, who was sitting near the door.
So he greeted Marlowe, who motioned him
To sit down. Marlowe reached into his jerkin,
And then his doublet, and found a bezoar stone,
A groat and two farthings. So he flipped
A farthing, looked at it somewhat carefully,
And finally said, "I reckon this pint's on me."

Shakespeare took a draught and then remarked,
"Kit, I have to say I rather liked your piece
About a Jewish merchant living on an island –
The Jew of Malta, I think you called it.
It occurs to me I might write one in that vein,
Perhaps I'd call it *The Merchant of Venice*."

And Marlowe responded, "Oh, help yourself, Will.
And that reminds me, I read your play
Richard III, an interesting study of an evil king.
It tempts me to essay one of my own
About another disastrous king of that line, *Edward II*."

Then Shakespeare said, "A fair exchange, Kit.
And I suppose this next pint is mine."

II

T.S. Eliot looked at his watch.
As he approached *Les Deux Moines*,
He knew he was fifteen minutes late
And feared Pound's well known temper.
But, no, the absinthe was on the table
And Pound was in a decent mood.

It had been ten years since
They had last been here together.
Eliot, thinking to please, greeted
Pound in Italian and Pound responded
In German. And so they talked
In various tongues, of the old days
Of Hemingway and Fitzgerald,
And Stein and all the rest
Of the American colony in Paris.

And they turned, of course,
To poetry and other arts.
They quoted Homer, Virgil and Ovid
And deplored the current works of poetry,
Nothing much since Tennyson and Browning
And, perhaps some bits of Whitman and Dickinson,
But plenty of defects there too.
They'd have to start a modern school
And get rid of all that subjective slop.

And then on to the state of the world.

Pound: The allies are confused and undisciplined.

Eliot: Yes, it is a *wasteland* out there.

Pound: We need a strong unifying leader, like Benito.

Eliot: And today we have only *hollow men.*

Pound: The trouble is the international bankers –
　　　　Of course, it's the Jews behind it all.

Eliot: Well, now I have to resent your bias.

Pound: And where do you find any bias?

Eliot: Why, clearly you forget that I was formerly a *banker.*

III

When Dante left this mortal life
He found himself in an afterworld.
And, wandering in it, he met a man –
A man he thought he recognized –
It clearly was Roman Virgil.
They met and walked together and conversed.

Virgil: I've been awaiting you these many years.

Dante: Yes, it's more than a millennium.

Virgil: I have one question I want to ask.

Dante: I'll surely give you an answer if I can.

Virgil: Why did you presume I'd be your guide
And go to all those dreadful places?

Dante: I thought I was honoring you, great sir,
To be my leader throughout the Inferno.

Virgil: If there ever is another time,
Consult me before you misuse my name.
I admit that, as a Roman, I was pleased
That you placed my great Aeneas,
A Trojan and founder of Rome, in
Your highest layer, which you called Limbo.
But I feel you slighted mighty Homer
When you sent his Ulysses and other Greeks
To nearly the deepest circle of your Inferno.
Homer is rather miffed, you know.

Dante: But Ulysses was an immoral man.

Virgil: You presume to sit in judgment on the whole world.

Dante: But you don't understand sin.
You're still just a pagan, you must admit.

Virgil: And you can just go to hell.

Dante: But that's where we are – the Inferno.

Virgil: No, where we are is Elysium –
The Elysian Isles, the Elysian Fields.
And I'm not sure that you belong here.

Invitation

Oh come, my dears, oh come with me,
Down to my grotto in the sea
And listen to the mermaids play
Their spiral conchs the livelong day.

And hear the liquid harmonies
Of coral and anemones,
Which serve as live retaining walls
For hoary Neptune's spacious halls.

My cavern's splashed with sparkling hints
Of blue and silver aquatints,
Although, in sun, you may behold
Gouaches of the finest gold.

Come hear the constant soothing sound
Of lapping wavelets all around.
Come dine with me on shrimp and crab;
Then hail a squid for taxicab.

Dr. Esperanzo

A man named Dr. Esperanzo came to our town.
He rented the old vacant Elm Street church,
 Put up posters for what he called
A "Free and All-revealing, Sermon-Lecture"
He called it "Speaking of God".
And on the Wednesday night he'd picked,
A couple of hundred people came to hear.
Of course I went along with all the rest.

Esperanzo was tall and thin and wore a beard.
He began by telling us to close our eyes
And bow our heads, relax and meditate.
And then in a deep voice, he began to speak.
I can recall part of what he said.
I thought it was pretty interesting
Even if it was somewhat irreligious.
So I've set out his talk as well as I can

Dr. Esperanzo said things like this:
He said he could understand why
The church was vacant. He said
Religion is the biggest hoax there is.
He said it was the cause of wars
And killing among all the people
Around the whole world.

He said some men seized all the
Churches and made themselves their rulers,
Leaving out the women and people
Who didn't look like them,
Or spoke different languages.
He said the world just happened,
Due to the effect of laws of nature.
It wasn't created by an old man with a beard.

He said Jesus and Mohammed were just
Gifted leaders, like him, who went around
Trying to tell people the truth
About the world as they saw it.
He said folks tell you that God
Created Man in his own image
But said the truth is that *Man*
Created *God* in *his* own image
And men should honor the Ideal Man
Who lives in everybody's brain…
And that's as far as Esperanzo got.

At the start, folks had seemed in a kind of trance,
But then some began to mutter and complain,
A few began to stir and shout things out.
And move about the back of the church.
Finally there was quite a commotion and disturbance.
Then some man came forward to the front
And, pretty soon, quite a large bunch.
I noticed Father Cassidy was with them.

Well, there was a kind of struggle and then
They rushed Dr. Esperanzo out of the church.
I couldn't quite see, but I am told
They put him on a rail and rode him
Out of town. He never came again.
Some of us thought this wasn't all just right
But somehow, we couldn't do anything in time…
That week the sign in front of Pastor Raymond's church
Said: "Sunday Sermon – The Lessons of Intolerance"
I planned to go, but, unfortunately, I got sick.
Afterward, I heard the sermon was quite good.

Neanderthals

Our science tells us much today,
Through relics of old caves,
Analysis of DNA
In bones from ancient graves.

Neanderthals of distant past,
Their bodies thick and strong,
Seemed built to flourish and to last –
But for the one thing wrong:

Their brains were of an equal size
To homo sapiens',
But, somehow, they were not as wise
Or quick as modern men's.

From DNA, beyond a doubt,
The species' interbred.
And, though Neanderthals died out,
Their hybrids were not dead;

Their offspring linger. As a rule,
We meet one every day –
The sluggish, dense and stubborn fool
Who can't see things our way.

The Salesman

I sold a house quite near Yellowstone Park –
    Hot water in the living room every four hours.
I sold a Ford that probably will last forever –
    Already has 400,000 miles on it.
I sold a suit that looks like an Armani –
    If you hold the lapels just right.
I sold a house with a great view of the Pacific –
    On the edge of a cliff in California.
I sold the whole remaining stock of Senior Pills –
    After the inventor died at thirty-two.
Being on a roll I asked Jill to marry me –
    She said, "No thanks…And what's the catch?"

The Muse's Call

In ages past there seemed a muse
Who would inspire or call and warn
A genius of time's flick'ring fuse
Or coming of a fate forlorn,

Who augured Schubert's lot austere,
Or Mozart's early death disclosed,
Or told Beethoven he'd not hear
The finest works he had composed.

Foretold Lord Byron's fatal fight
Or Shelley's quick demise – or Keats',
Or Milton that he'd lose his sight –
Thus speeding genius to new feats.

It's mine to ponder and bemoan
That muses from past history
Could not pick up the telephone
And rouse some genius out of me.

Identity Crisis

I'm beginning to think
I may be a real corporeal object
That other people can see.

In a group photo I can pick out
A figure that I say is me,
But what do I really look like?

In the mirror I see an image;
I can adjust the image's necktie,
But does the image occupy
A space in the real world?

When I play my answering machine,
I hear a voice. Does it belong
To a real person I call me?
Am I there? Am I here?
I *think* I think;
Therefore I *think* I am.

Love Will Never Die

Hey, pretty lady, you're my newfound dream.
You make my dentures loudly clash and clack.
You obfuscate my trifocals with steam;
You almost renovate my aching back.
My hearing aids well-nigh explode with sound.
I quite forget my creaking rheumatiz,
My fallen arches rise and leave the ground
When you and I encounter phiz to phiz.

For you, I'll take my every blasted pill:
My Lasix, Lipitor and Librium,
My Prozac, Prilosec and Prinivil,
My Lactaid, Levaquin and Lithium.
And you can bet I'll stay on my Cialis
For upkeep of my antiquated . . . palace?

Let it Go

Hey, let it go, man!
Let it all hang out.
What you saving it for?
Who you saving it for?
I suppose you're
Saving it for posterity?
Posterity is here, man.
Posterity is right now!

Sure, I know,
You're just a kid –
A promising kid.
You saving it for
When you grow up?
That better be soon –
Your birth certificate
Says 1919.

Telephone Dialogue

Grandpa: Hi, buddy, how ya doing?

Teenager: Ok, I guess.

GP: What you been up to lately?

TA: Nuthin'.

GP: Been having any fun?

TA: Not really.

GP: How's school?

TA: It's ok, I s'pose.

GP: What's your favorite thing in school?

TA: Like – recess.

GP: What's your favorite sport?

TA: I'm not doing sports.

GP: Well, what do you do when you're not in school?

TA: Like, you know, hang out.

GP: Your birthday's coming up. What would you like for
a present?

TA: I dunno.

GP: A check, I suppose?

TA: They're kind of a drag. Mom has to cash them –

GP: Maybe some folding money, then?

TA: Ok, I guess.

GP: How much do you need?

TA: I dunno. It's your call.

GP: Well, I'll do something. Anyway, it's sure been nice
talking to you.

TA: Yeah. Me too.

Two Pets

I have a rather ugly dog.
His name is Akhenaten.
He worships but a single god.
Indeed, he worships me!

I have a very graceful cat.
Her name is Nefertiti.
She worships but a single god.
Alas, her god is she!

The First to Go

The first to go
Of every part
It's good to know
Is not the heart.

It's not a lung
And not a hand.
It's not the tongue
Nor yet a gland.

I've tested all
But now I find
The first to fall,
I call my mind.

Seaside

I perch upon my seaside porch
And doze and dream beneath the sun,
'Mid soporific sounds of seas,
Relentless roaring of the surf;
The furious foam atop the waves
That wear their whitecaps jauntily.

The crests must crash in booming bursts
And then slide up the silver sand,
In fan-shaped floes or florid forms;
But backslide down the beach again,
Rejoining furrows following,
To surge and slide as surf once more.

Progression

With time we turn from –

Impulse to Reflection
Neglect to Memory
The Body to the Mind

Denial to Acceptance
Self to Sharing
Bias to Tolerance

Material to the Spiritual
Joy to Happiness
Heat to Light.

Beyond the Delta

My trip was long, the river slow,
I docked my craft at many ports,
But others passed, unvisited.
Through all my countless varied years,
I sailed alone and drifted far.
And now, at last, I reach the sea –
Beyond the delta's farthest sands –
And float the limitless unknown.

About the Author

*A*s this is published, David Ryrie Brink has just celebrated his 96th birthday. According to Brink, he has been a poet only since attaining the age of 88. So much for the view that poets must start young.

Brink was born of parents with distinguished literary achievements – his mother a noted writer of fiction and his father an eminent math professor and writer. As a young man, Brink rebelled a bit against entering the fields of writing and teaching. However, fate inexorably brought him back to both fields.

Brink decided to go to law school, as much as anything, to satisfy his curiosity as to what went on there. His law school studies were interrupted by World War II. The US Navy selected him for a secret program of cryptanalysis (breaking enemy codes and ciphers). As the war ended, he held the rank of Lieutenant Commander.

Upon finishing law school after the war he was offered jobs both teaching law and practising in a large firm. He finally chose the Dorsey law firm in Minneapolis. In due course he became the partner heading the Trusts and Estates practice. He became known as the dean of that practice in the Upper Midwest area, in large part through, yes, writing and teaching practising lawyers.

Among other distinctions, Brink was elected President of his local Bar Association, then the State Bar Association, and finally the American Bar Association with its 400,000 volunteer lawyer members. He received honorary doctorates or other honors from various universities and law schools and headed a number of law-related organizations.

Brink retired from his partnership at Dorsey at age 70 and began pursuing various professional and charitable activities. In 2007 he received one of those postcards that say "Write a Poem and Win a Prize". On a whim, he wrote a poem and sent it in. The postcard offer turned out to be a sham, but Brink had caught the poetry bug. He began to read and study poetry intensively, leading him to write poetry, to publish some, to teach poetry and to form poetry clubs. His writing and teaching finally came home to roost in poetry. Now he publishes some of his work in the form of *Beyond the Delta*.

It is a very fine read.

-David P. Murrin

CPSIA information can be obtained
at www.ICGtesting.com
Printed in the USA
FFOW01n0220120216
21407FF

9 781634 137638